MATH
ON THE JOB

Working in Sports

This could be you!

Rick Wunderlich

Crabtree Publishing Company
www.crabtreebooks.com

D1558314

LAND O'LAKES
BRANCH

Crabtree Publishing Company
www.crabtreebooks.com

Dedicated by Rick Wunderlich
To my son Paul, who loves sports and teaching math. If these books inspire children to pursue their dreams
and be the best they can be mathematically, they will have served their purpose.

Author: Rick Wunderlich

Editorial director: Kathy Middleton

Editors: Reagan Miller, Janine Deschenes, and
   Crystal Sikkens

Photo research: Margaret Amy Salter

Designer: Margaret Amy Salter

Proofreader: Kathy Middleton

Production coordinator and prepress technician:
   Margaret Amy Salter

Print coordinator: Katherine Berti

Math Consultant: Diane Dakers

Special thanks to Tom Berube

Photographs:
Icon Sportswire: Tony Quinn: p23; TMB: p25 (bottom right);
Shutterstock: © Jakkrit Orrasri: front cover (left middle), p22;
   © HodagMedia: title page, p29; © Jamie Roach: p6;
   © Alison Young: p9; © Eric Broder Van Dyke: p10;
   © Paolo Bona: p15; © Aspen Photo: p25 (top);
Creative Commons: Tony McCune: front cover (bottom
   center); Chris J. Nelson: p7
Public Domain: Nacho Anazawa: p4

All other images by Shutterstock

Library and Archives Canada Cataloguing in Publication

Wunderlich, Rick, author
    Math on the job : working in sports / Richard Wunderlich.

(Math on the job)
Includes index.
Issued in print and electronic formats.
ISBN 978-0-7787-2362-2 (bound).--
ISBN 978-0-7787-2371-4 (paperback).--
ISBN 978-1-4271-1743-4 (html)

    1. Sports--Mathematics--Juvenile literature. 2. Mathematics--
Juvenile literature. I. Title. II. Title: Working in sports.

GV705.4.W86 2016   j796.01'51   C2015-908048-7
                                        C2015-908049-5

Library of Congress Cataloging-in-Publication Data

Names: Wunderlich, Richard, author.
Title: Math on the job. Working in sports / Richard Wunderlich.
Other titles: Working in sports
Description: New York, New York : Crabtree Publishing Company,
   [2016] | Series: Math on the job | Includes index.
Identifiers: LCCN 2016002527 (print) | LCCN 2016004777 (ebook) |
   ISBN 9780778723622 (reinforced library binding : alk. paper) |
   ISBN 9780778723714 (pbk. : alk. paper) |
   ISBN 9781427117434 (electronic HTML)
Subjects: LCSH: Sports--Mathematics--Juvenile literature. |
   Mathematics--Juvenile literature.
Classification: LCC GV706.8 .W86 2016 (print) | LCC GV706.8 (ebook)
   | DDC 796--dc23
LC record available at http://lccn.loc.gov/2016002527

Crabtree Publishing Company
www.crabtreebooks.com   1-800-387-7650

Printed in Canada/022016/IH20151223

Copyright © **2016 CRABTREE PUBLISHING COMPANY.** All rights reserved. No part of this publication may be reproduced, stored in
a retrieval system or be transmitted in any form or by any means, electronic, mechanical, photocopying, recording, or otherwise, without the prior
written permission of Crabtree Publishing Company. In Canada: We acknowledge the financial support of the Government of Canada through the
Canada Book Fund for our publishing activities.

Published in Canada
Crabtree Publishing
616 Welland Ave.
St. Catharines, ON
L2M 5V6

Published in the United States
Crabtree Publishing
PMB 59051
350 Fifth Avenue, 59th Floor
New York, New York 10118

Published in the United Kingdom
Crabtree Publishing
Maritime House
Basin Road North, Hove
BN41 1WR

Published in Australia
Crabtree Publishing
3 Charles Street
Coburg North
VIC 3058

Contents

Please note:
The standard and metric systems are used
interchangeably throughout this book.

Professional Sports

Being involved in professional **sports is exciting, interesting, and challenging. Many children dream of becoming a professional athlete, but there are many other interesting jobs within the field of professional sports.**

Imagine you are a baseball player, and you have been invited to a professional baseball team's training camp. You know the coaches will be watching you. You wonder if you'll perform well enough to be considered a **prospect**.

There are also opportunities for sports fans. They know the players and the game, and keep up-to-date on **data** from recent sports games.

There are ways to use your talents to help the team off the field. You could become the team statistician! Your job is to track the team's performance, watch for promising players, and use mathematics to give the team management an advantage. Your work helps build the team!

Are you a fan of many different sports? How would you like to be a professional sports journalist? You would watch the games, then interview coaches and players afterward to get the story behind the big wins and heartbreaking losses. What amazing ways to earn a living!

CAREER 1

PROFESSIONAL BASEBALL PLAYER

Some baseball players spend much of their childhood on the baseball diamond. As they get older, the game can become more competitive and only the top players may be chosen to join "All-Star" teams.

Top players who are graduating from high school may be invited to show off their skills at **scouting camps**. At these camps, **scouts** from college and university teams come to look for prospects, or promising players, who may be talented enough to play for their teams.

Think Like a Baseball Prospect

Some colleges and universities offer **athletic scholarships** to top prospects to play for their teams.

Imagine you are a talented baseball pitcher. You get invited to a scouting camp to show off your pitching skills to college and university scouts.

Pitch speed is the main thing that scouts measure and compare when searching for the best pitcher prospects. Other things measured include the numbers of strikes and walks a pitcher throws.

Baseball scouts use **radar guns** to measure the speed of a pitcher's **fastball** at a scouting camp.

SOLVE:

You throw five fastballs, and a scout measures the speed of each pitch. The scout wants to find out the average speed of your pitches. To find the average, she adds together the speeds of each pitch, then divides the sum by the number of pitches you threw.

The scout records your average pitch speed is 80 miles per hour. Do you agree with the scout's calculations? Why or why not?

PITCH NUMBER	SPEED IN MILES PER HOUR
1	78
2	81
3	82
4	79
5	80

When a player is "up to bat," they stand at home plate and attempt to hit a baseball that is coming toward them, sometimes faster than 100 miles per hour (mph). Since the pitcher is about 60 feet from home plate, the batter only has a fraction of a second to see the ball and decide whether to swing or not. If the pitch is 90 mph, the ball takes 0.4 seconds to reach the batter!

After hitting the ball, the batter must make it to first base before the ball gets there. Baseball scouts will often measure how fast a prospect can run to first base after hitting the ball.

Scouts analyze the data about players in order to find players who are good enough to play for a college or professional team. One skill to practice is estimation. Estimation is using rounding to make calculations more simple.

When rounding values, look at the last number to determine whether to round up or down. If the final number is 5 or above, round up. If the final number is 4 or below, round down. For example: 4.6 rounds to 5, and 4.3 rounds to 4.

The opposing team catches and throws the ball to the first baseman. The first baseman must catch the ball with a foot on the base.

For example, if you estimate
3.14 x 5.85
you might round
3.14 to 3
and
5.85 to 6.
3 x 6 = 18.

ANALYZE:

1 A prospect made it to first base in 4.8 seconds after hitting the ball. The distance from home plate to first base is 90 feet. Use rounding to help estimate how many feet the runner traveled in 1 second. Scouts use information like this to rate players from being an excellent prospect to a poor prospect. A good scout looks at this data and makes recommendations to college and professional team coaches.

2 The distance between the bases is 90 feet. Perimeter is the length of the path around an object. What is the perimeter of the path a runner takes to touch all four bases?

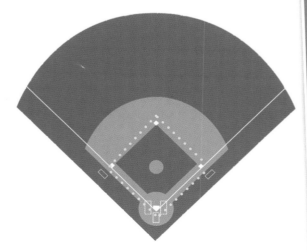

A batter's box has an area of 24 square feet. If the length of the batter's box is 6 feet, what is the width of the box? Remember, area = length × width. Use any method you wish, such as trial and error, to find what width fits a rectangle with a length of 6 feet and an area of 24 feet. This is important for batters because if a batter steps out of the batter's box during a pitch, the umpire will penalize them with a strike.

DECIDE:

Left-handed batters have an advantage over right-handed batters. One advantage is that the batter's box used by left-handed batters is sightly closer to first base, so these players have a shorter distance to run. Another advantage is that, especially in the younger leagues, there are more right-handed pitchers than left-handed pitchers. Because of the way hitting a ball works, it is much easier for a left-handed batter to hit a ball thrown by a right-handed pitcher.

As a young player, you can decide that you want to learn to hit left-handed or even become a "switch hitter," who can bat from either side. Being able to hit from both sides makes you a better prospect.

RATING	RIGHT-HANDED BATTER (seconds to run to first base)	LEFT-HANDED BATTER (seconds to run to first base)
Above average	4.5	4.4
Average	4.6	4.5
Below Average	4.7	4.6
Poor	4.8	4.7

1 Looking at the table above, what do you notice about the differences between batting left and batting right?

2 Would it make sense to spend time learning to bat left if you are naturally right-handed? Why or why not?

In baseball, there is more than one way of getting to first base. One way is to get a base hit. A base hit happens when a batter hits a ball and gets to first base without being tagged "out" by the first baseman.

Another way of getting to first base is by getting a "walk." This means the pitcher threw 4 pitches that were outside of the area known as the strike zone, and the batter did not swing at them. The strike zone is an area over home plate that is between a batter's shoulders and knees. A tougher way to get to first base is to be accidentally struck by a pitch.

Baseball **statistics** often include the **batting average** of the players. A batting average measures how many times a player is likely to get a hit. It is reported as a 3 digit decimal. For example, a player who gets a hit every third time at bat has an average of 1/3 or .333. A batting average this high is amazing!

STRIKE ZONE

TOUGH DECISION:

Imagine you are a scout at a scouting camp. You have been watching two pitcher prospects. One prospect can throw the ball at 98 mph and has a batting average of 0.098. The other pitcher can throw the ball at 93 mph and has a batting average of 0.157. Which prospect would you be more interested in and why?

FRACTIONS TO DECIMALS

To convert batting data to a batting average, use the formula shown in the example below.

Suppose a batter has been to bat 80 times and has gotten a base hit 20 times.

First, convert the data to a fraction: $\dfrac{20}{80}$

Then, divide the numerator by the denominator:

$20 \div 80 = 0.25$

Since batting averages are reported as 3 decimal places, 0.25 becomes .250.

NAME: Tom Berube
POSITION: Baseball pitcher

How is math important in your career?

As a fastball pitcher, I need to use math to determine how fast I am throwing pitches. I need to know the miles per hour that my pitches are traveling, and the meters per second the baseball covers. Using math to figure these numbers out helps me practice to set goals for my pitching speed against opposing players who are good batters. I also use math to estimate where the ball needs to be thrown. I need to have good **spatial** awareness, so that I can accurately throw the ball inside the strike zone. I estimate the area, in meters squared, of each batter's strike zone, so I know how much space I have to target the zone.

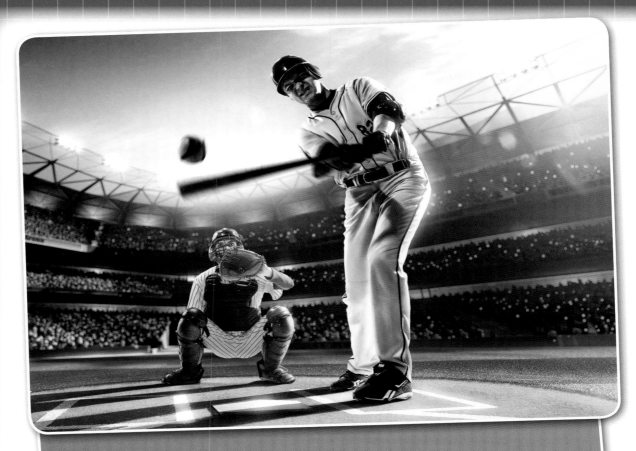

WANT TO BE A PROFESSIONAL BASEBALL PLAYER?

1. Join a local baseball team, or volunteer to help coach a little league team in your neighborhood.

2. Read all you can about baseball. Online sources such as ESPN (espn.go.com) can help you keep up to date.

3. Follow local sports teams by going to the games and reading what the writers say in news sources.

CAREER
PATHWAYS

This could be you!

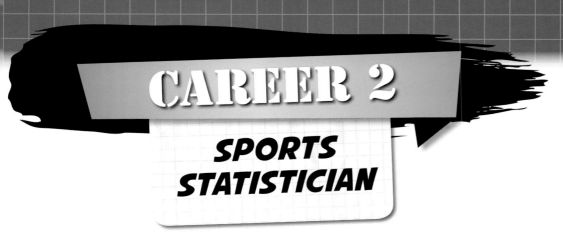

CAREER 2

SPORTS STATISTICIAN

If you love sports, and you love math, this may be the career for you!

A sports statistician collects statistics related to basketball, baseball, golf, track, and other team and individual sports. Statistics are numbers that describe the standings, or rankings, of players and teams in different categories. The statistics collected vary by sport, but may include categories such as wins, losses, penalties, attempted shots, and assists. Statistics can be used in different ways by different people. For example, athletes might use statistics to track how well they are playing and identify areas in which they can improve. Coaches might use statistics to determine which plays work best against different teams. Being a sports statistician can be a rewarding and exciting job. What could be more fun than watching great athletes do what they do best? Then, you get to use math to find out ways to help a team or player.

Think Like a Sports Statistician

Imagine you are a sports statistician working with Susan, who is a professional golfer. Susan wants you to look for patterns in her scores that might be hurting her game. One way you could do this is by collecting data on her scores for different holes. A hole is one unit of the golf course's entire length. The entire course is 18 holes. You could find out which holes she has trouble with, and make recommendations on how to improve her game.

You read over Susan's golf scores and focus on the holes that she struggled on. You can tell which holes she struggled with by how many **strokes** she took to complete it. Too many strokes gives you a high score. A player needs to take as few strokes as possible to sink a ball, so the lower the score the better.

FACTS:

"Par" in golf is a measure of how many strokes a good player should take to sink the ball in a particular hole. The longer distance a golf hole is, the higher the par will be. For example, a par of 5 means that players should take five strokes to get the ball in the hole. A score of par is a good goal. A score less than par is very good, and a score greater than par is bad for a golfer.

SOLVE:

1 You look at Susan's scorecards over several months and find her average scores for three types of holes: short (par 3), medium (par 4), and long (par 5).

Here are her results:

PAR FOR THE HOLE	SUSAN'S AVERAGE NUMBER OF STROKES
3	2.8
4	4.1
5	5.2

a) Describe how a golfer could get an average that includes a portion of a stroke. In other words, how is it possible to get a score that is a decimal? Show using an example. Look back to page 8 to remember how to calculate an average.

b) Look at the average scores. Which type of hole (short, medium, or long) does Susan play the best? Explain how you know.

2 You and Susan decide to work on a strategy for the par-4 holes first. Golf professionals recommend the length of a par-4 hole for women is anywhere from 211 to 400 yards.

TABLE A

HOLE LENGTH (yards)	221-274 (SHORT)	275-338 (MEDIUM)	339-400 (LONG)
Average number of strokes	3.8	4.1	4.3

a) What length is halfway between 211 and 400 yards? Show your work.

b) You decide to group her scores for par-4 holes into 3 groups, depending on the hole's length. The table above shows the results of your work. Which length of par-4 holes does Susan need improvement on? How do you know?

DECIDE: You have collected and studied the data. You have created a table (labeled Table A on page 17) to show Susan's strong and weak points when playing a par 4 hole. Susan asks you to put this information into a graph so she can see where she is struggling more clearly. You have to decide which type of graph would be the easiest for Susan to study the data.

Would you choose to use a **pictograph** or a bar graph to show Table A? Create a graph that visually shows the pattern that is seen in table A.

Looking at a graph shows that her game gets worse as the hole gets longer. A graph also shows that her score is getting much closer to 5, which is not good for a golfer on a par-4 hole. From the graph, Susan can see where she needs extra practice.

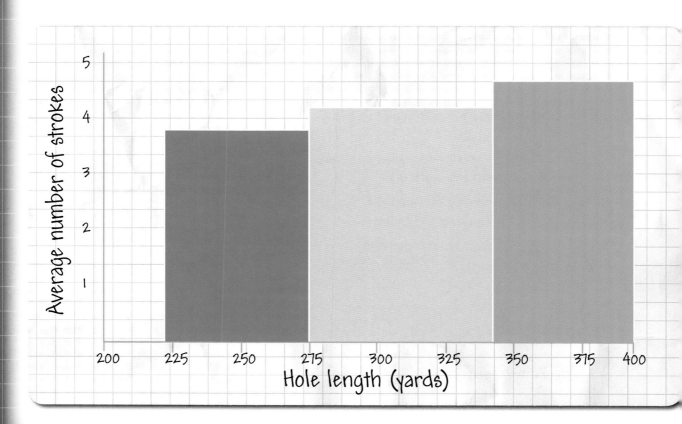

ANALYZE:

Susan is pleased with the job you did collecting and presenting the data on her par 4 scores. She has now asked if you would analyze her **putting**. She wants you to look for a pattern in the way she putts in different situations, and give her some guidance about how to adjust her game.

One way you could try to help Susan with her putting is to look at the type of putter she uses, and experiment with different styles of putters.

small head

You start the experiment by having Susan play 10 rounds of golf with her regular putter and record the number of putts she made. Then, have her play 10 rounds with each of the 3 putters shown at right.

You find the average of her putts over the 10 rounds using each of the 4 putter styles and put the data in the table below. Susan can then see how each putter affected her number of putts. Remember that in golf, the fewer the putts the better!

medium head

Use the data below to draw a bar graph so Susan can see the results more clearly. Which type of putter helped Susan's game? How do you know?

large head

PUTTER TYPE	AVERAGE PUTTS OVER 10 ROUNDS
regular putter	73
small-head putter	72
medium-head putter	73
large-head putter	68

MATH TOOLBOX

GRAPHING DISTANCE

Graphs are a great way of presenting numbers so that people can see patterns in them. Look at the graph below. It shows how the speed of the golf club affects how far the ball goes.

For example, from the graph, a golfer can see that increasing the speed you swing from 90 to 100 mph changes the distance the ball goes by about 20 yards.

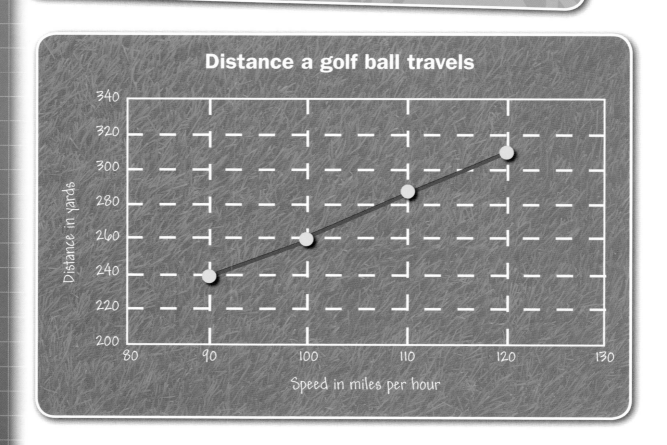

Distance a golf ball travels

Distance in yards (y-axis: 200, 220, 240, 260, 280, 300, 320, 340)

Speed in miles per hour (x-axis: 80, 90, 100, 110, 120, 130)

This could be you!

WANT TO BE A SPORTS STATISTICIAN?

1. Stay in school! A great education with a focus on math is a good beginning. Take college courses such as probability and statistics in order to understand how to use statistics. Most colleges offer these courses.

2. Visit your school guidance counselor or local library and ask about information about statistics.

3. Read all you can about sports. Online sources such as ESPN (espn.go.com) are great ways to keep up to date. Learn which "stats" are important to various sports and read what professionals have to say about using them.

4. Follow local sports teams by going to the games and reading what the writters say in news sources.

CAREER PATHWAYS

CAREER 3

SPORTS JOURNALIST

Becoming a sports journalist, or writer, is a great way to combine your love for sports with a career. Some journalists follow a particular sport, and travel with the teams to search for interesting stories. Others write the text for sports commentators to read on television or radio.

Think Like a Sports Journalist

Imagine you are working for a major sports channel. You have been given an assignment to write a story about women's basketball. You do some research and decide to write a story about professional basketball player Kara Lawson.

The information below was taken from ESPN's website.

Kara Marie Lawson (born February 14, 1981) is an American professional women's basketball player in the Women's National Basketball Association (WNBA) and a women's basketball television analyst for ESPN. Lawson primarily plays as a shooting guard. She won a gold medal at the 2008 Olympics in Beijing, China. Lawson joined the Connecticut Sun for the 2010 season as a free agent [not under contract with a team] and remained with the team through the 2013 season. She was traded to the Washington Mystics in the 2013-14 off-season.

High school

Lawson attended Sidwell Friends School her freshman year, then went to West Springfield High School, where she played on the girls' basketball and soccer teams. Lawson was named a WBCA All-American. She participated in the 1999 WBCA High School All-America Game, where she scored twenty points and earned MVP honors.

College

Lawson attended the University of Tennessee (UT) and played for the Lady Vols basketball team, coached by Pat Summitt. She enrolled in UT's College of Business, and graduated in 2003 with a degree in Finance. Lawson received the Frances Pomeroy Naismith Award from the Women's Basketball Coaches Association as the best senior player under 5 ft 8 in (1.7 m).

LEGEND

GP	Games played	**BPG**	Blocks per game	**PPG**	Points per game
FG%	Field goal percentage	**3P%**	3-point field goal percentage	**FT%**	Free throw percentage
RPG	Rebounds per game	**APG**	Assists per game	**SPG**	Steals per game

YEAR	TEAM	GP	POINTS	FG%	3P%	FT%	RPG	APG	SPG	BPG	PPG
1999-00	Tennessee	37	504	45.8	43.6	81.7	4.1	2.8	1.4	0.2	13.6
2000-01	Tennessee	34	386	43.3	41.3	85.7	3.5	3.3	1.0	0.1	11.4
2001-02	Tennessee	34	512	46.6	33.0	83.5	4.9	2.6	1.4	0.1	15.1
2002-03	Tennessee	38	548	46.9	45.0	88.4	4.9	4.0	1.1	0.2	14.4
Career	Tennessee	143	1950	45.8	41.5	84.7	4.3	3.2	1.2	0.1	13.6

You plan to incorporate Kara's game statistics into your article. Using the chart above, answer the following questions to build interesting statistics for your article.

SOLVE:

1 How many games did Kara play in total from 1999 to 2003?

2 What year did Kara have the lowest rebounds per game (RPG)?

3 Look at her APG (assists per game) results. What year was her best in earning assists per game?

An assist in basketball means that a player passes the ball to another player who then takes a shot and scores a basket.

ANALYZE:

1 What year was Kara's best for overall points? What year was her worst?

2 In the season 2001/2002, Kara had the highest average for points per game. The next year her total points increased, but her average points per game dropped. Explain how that is possible.

DECIDE:

Some might say that, in the 2000-01 season, the reason Kara's yearly point total was low was because she only played in 34 games.

Do you agree with that statement? What evidence do you see in the statistics that supports your conclusion?

PRACTICE WRITING:

Suppose you decide to write a story entitled "Kara Lawson, her years with Tennessee." Look at the table of statistics on page 24. Review the statistics for each year. In which categories was 2002-2003 her best year?

One of the best things you can do to learn how to write sports articles is to practice. Using the statistics in the table on page 24, write a paragraph about Kara Lawson. Include the following statistics in your article:

> The year in which she contributed the most points from the free throw line

> The year in which she played the most games

> The year in which she scored the most three-point baskets

MATH TOOLBOX

PATTERNS

Reading tables of statistics can be challenging, but it is crucial to sports journalism. Journalists must interpret tables of numbers in order to come up with interesting and accurate stories.

Look for patterns, such as low or high results over a period of time, changes in results, and changes that appear to be tied to a particular cause, such as the number of games played.

WANT TO BE A SPORTS JOURNALIST?

1. Stay in school! A great education with a lot of math and language arts courses is the key.

2. Play a lot of sports at school and join teams when you can.

3. Volunteer to write for your school newspaper if possible.

4. Visit your school guidance counselor or local library and ask about colleges that offer journalism programs.

CAREER PATHWAYS

This could be you!

Learning More

Websites

Time for kids is a magazine designed for youth. Learn how you can become a TFK sports reporter!
www.sikids.com/kid-reporter

In this video, an assistant general manager from a MLB (Major League Baseball) team explains the role of stats and other math in team operations:

www.pbslearningmedia.org/resource/mkaet.math.sp.baseball/real-life-math-baseball/

Books

Adamson, Thomas, K. *Baseball: The Math of the Game*. Capstone Press, 2012.

Braun, Eric. *Baseball Stats and the Stories Behind Them: What Every Fan Needs to Know*. Capstone Press, 2016.

Editors at Sports Illustrated Kids. *Sports Illustrated Kids STATS!: The Greatest Number in Sports*. Sports Illustrated, 2013.

Raymos, Rick. *STEM Jobs In Sports*. STEM Jobs You'll Love Series: Rourke Publishing, 2014.

ANSWERS

Career 1: Professional Baseball Player

Solve: The scout is correct. The math proves the average speed is
$$(78 + 81 + 82 + 79 + 80) \div 5 = 80 \text{ mph.}$$

Analyze: 1. Rounding 4.8 to 5, the prospect ran approximately
90 feet ÷ 5 feet = 18 feet per second.

2. The perimeter of the path touching all bases is 90 feet × 4 bases = 360 feet.

Box text: The width of the batter's box is 24 square feet ÷ 6 feet = 4 feet.

Decide: 1. Left-handed batters can run to first base in 0.1 seconds faster than right-handed batters.

2. The data suggests it is worth learning to bat left because you can get to first base more quickly, increasing your chance of being safe on first.

Tough Decision: If your team mostly needs a fast pitcher, go with the first prospect.
If your team mostly needs a reliable hitter, go with the second prospect.

Glossary

athletic scholarship An opportunity given to attend a college, based on a student's athletic ability

batting average The number of hits divided by the number of times the player is at bat

data Factual information in numbers, used for reasoning or calculations

estimation The act of making a reasonable guess or judgement

fastball A baseball pitch thrown at full speed

home plate A rubber plate set on a baseball field, marking the start and end points of baseball runs

pictograph A way to organize information using pictures to represent data; For example, a golf club could represent one stroke taken at a hole.

probability In mathematics, a measurement of the likelihood of an event

professional The status of a person who earns money through their activities

prospect In sports, a player who has potential to play at a professional level

putting In golf, a light stroke on the putting green in an attempt to get the ball in a hole

radar gun A device used to measure the speed of something, such as a baseball pitch

scouting camp A place where professional sports personnel invite prospects in order to judge their potential as players

scouts People sent out to find new, talented athletes

spatial Relating to space

statistics A list of numerical facts

strokes In golf, the act of hitting a ball by swinging a golf club at it

ANSWERS CONTINUED
Career 2: Sports Statistician

Solve: 1. a) An average number often contains decimals because you are dividing numbers into small parts. For example, if Susan's scores on par 3-holes were 2, 3, 2, 4, and 3, the sum would be 14. Then, divide the sum by the number of scores, which is 5. The average is 2.8.

b) Susan does best playing par-3 holes, or short holes, because her average is less than par.

2. a) The difference between guideline lengths for a par 4 is 400 – 211 = 189 yards. Half that length is 189 ÷ 2 = 94.5. Add that to the lower guideline to get the halfway mark bewteen the two points: 211 + 94.5 = 305.5 yards,

b) Susan needs improvement on medium and long holes because her average on these holes is over par.

Decide: A bar graph would probably be better to show how Susan's scores slowly increase as the length of the par 4 increases.

Analyze: A putter with a large head would help Susan's game because her putting average was the lowest using a large-head putter.

Index

ANSWERS CONTINUED

Career 3: Sports Journalist

Solve: 1. Kara played 143 games.

2. Her lowest RPG was in 2000/2001.

3. 2002/2003 was her best in assists per game.

Analyze: 1. Her best year for points was 2002/2003. Her worst was 2000/2001.

2. Kara had a few high-scoring games which caused her total points to increase, but she had several games in which she scored very few points which caused her average points per game to decrease.

Decide: No, I don't agree with the statement because her points per game also dropped, and she only played 34 games the next season and her total points were much higher.

Practice Writing: 2002-2003 was Kara's best year in all categories except SPG and PPG.

Author Bio:

Rick Wunderlich loves how math and sports are so related. Rick has written math and science textbooks and has had the best job in the world for him, a teacher. He also tips his hat to imaginary spectators when he makes a good golf shot.